Helps, Hints and Hope

For the Homework-Weary Among Us

~~~~~~~~~~

Miriam C. Owens

"...My grace is sufficient for you, for my power is made perfect in weakness"

2 Corinthians 12:9
~~~~~~~~~~

Published by Rhema Designs, LLC
PO Box 85
Mechanicsville, VA 23111

Cover Design by: Stephen Callender

Library of Congress Control Number: 2012913272

ISBN-10: 0615662587
ISBN-13: 978-0-615-66258-9

Printed in the United States of America

Dedication

This book is dedicated to my family.

Russell: God could not have blessed me with a more suitable and perfect mate! Thank you so much for loving me unconditionally and for patiently supporting me as I've pursued my dreams.

And to my children…

Alicia: It has been my honor and my pleasure to watch you mature into a capable, intelligent and loving young adult. Even now, as you continue with your academic pursuits at the college level, I still smile each time you call or stop by to ask me for my views and opinions on your school assignments. You make me proud!

Anthony: Stay true to yourself and to God. Your strong sense of determination has served you well, and will continue to propel you to new heights. Remember to keep God close as you soar to those new heights, allowing Him to direct each of your paths. I am proud to be your mom!

Sarah: I am so proud of you! Continue to do your best in everything you do. When things get a little difficult, remember that you have a loving God and a supportive family who are with you every step of the way! Never be afraid to take on a challenge. With God all things are possible.

I love you all immensely….

Mom

Table of Contents

Appendices

If one were to ask the parents of school-aged children to name an area of parenting difficulty they wish they had practical ideas and solutions for, homework frustration would be a likely response from many of them. Narrow the scope a bit and pose the same question to parents of school-aged children with learning differences and intellectual challenges. An overwhelming majority of these parents would probably admit that the nightly struggle surrounding the completion of their children's homework assignments is near the top of their list of daily stressors.

Completing homework can be a challenge for just about any student from time to time, but it can be especially difficult for students with unique learning styles. My personal experiences as the mother of a child with learning differences inspired me to write this book. *Helps, Hints and Hope* is a book about possibility, rather than impossibility. It is a book that will help to strengthen your faith while offering you practical, common-sense solutions to academic challenges that your child may be experiencing. *Helps, Hints and Hope* will help you to appreciate yourself and your child for the wonderfully unique and talented individuals that you are!

Peace and blessings,

Miriam

Disclaimer

This book is to be used as a guide. It was written to serve as a source of information and ideas only. It should not, under any circumstances, be used as a substitute for the professional advice of the subject's physician or professional advisor. The information in this book should not be interpreted as advice. The author is not engaged in the rendering of psychological, financial, or other professional services. If professional assistance is needed, the services of a competent professional should be sought. The author shall not be liable or responsible to any person or entity with respect to any loss or damage caused, or alleged to be caused, directly or indirectly, by the information and ideas contained in this book.

Introduction

"Helps, Hints and Hope" is a book that will help you as you seek to empower your child academically. It is not a book filled with "one size fits all" solutions but, rather, a book that will show you how to discover your child's unique needs and strengths. Once you've accomplished this, you will learn how to employ practical, common-sense strategies that will play to your child's strengths while taking his unique educational, emotional and physical needs into consideration.

As with the use of any other interventions or strategies, using the ideas from this book will require investments of both time and patience. My daughter and I have used many of the ideas and techniques described in the book with a very consistent degree of success. Keep in mind, however, that your child is unique. Consequently, you may find it necessary to make slight adjustments to some of the suggested strategies to make them as appropriate and personal for your child as possible.

The ideas and suggestions offered in *"Helps, Hints and Hope"* assume that readers have already taken the steps necessary to ensure that their children have educational plans in place which are both effective *and* appropriate. If you have not taken these steps and believe that your child's current educational plan is *not* effective or appropriate, you should consider reaching out to your child's teacher or principal to voice your concerns. (See Appendix A for a sample letter that you can use to do this.)

Chapter One: Take Time to Reflect and Assess

"For I know the plans I have for you, says the Lord. They are plans for good...to give you a future and a hope" Jeremiah 29:11 (TLB)

As a parent or caregiver, you probably know your child better than anyone else. After all, you've witnessed most, if not all, of his "firsts": his first breath, his first smile, his first teeth, his first steps, etc. Do you remember how proud you were with the acquisition of each new skill or the passing of each milestone? Well, of course you do! You've made countless sacrifices to make sure that your child was loved and properly cared for. You've been there for all of the joys and sorrows that have touched your child's life, and probably wouldn't trade those memories for anything!

Your intimate knowledge of your child makes you an expert on the subject of your child. Your thoughts, feelings and opinions *about* him play a vitally important role in shaping your interactions *with* him. For example, if you know that your child is extremely sensitive, the words that you use to speak to him are usually shaped by your presumption(s) of how he will respond to what you have to say. How many times have you had to stop and re-think how you would verbally deliver a message to your already frustrated son or daughter because you knew how "touchy" or "defensive" he or she would become when they heard it? How often have you found yourself "padding" family discussions that involved your child, most likely in a subconscious attempt to preempt any negative verbalizations or behaviors that you were sure would result from your child's misunderstanding of the discussion?

A "padded" family discussion might begin like this:

Dad: "Son, didn't I ask you to take the garbage out over an hour ago?

Son: "Sure, dad. I'll get to it."

Dad: "I want you to stop what you're doing and take the garbage out right now!"

Son: (now visibly upset because his father has raised his voice) "Okay, okay! You don't have to yell!"

Dad: "I'm yelling because you never follow directions!"

Enter Mom...

Mom understands that their son's difficulties with focus and attention sometimes make it difficult, if not impossible, for him to attend to more than one activity at a time. She realizes that her son may not have even heard his father's initial request to take out the garbage because he was playing his favorite video game when his father began speaking to him. She instinctively jumps into their conversation before it escalates any further to provide the emotional "padding" that will be necessary for father and son to communicate calmly and effectively. Let's listen in.

Mom: (directing her comment toward her son) "Please pause your video game and look at me for a moment." She waits until she has her son's undivided attention. It takes him a full 15 seconds to comply with her request to look at her, but she waits patiently, understanding that he may have needed a little extra time to process her request and transition from playing the video game to looking at her. When she has his attention, she speaks to him again with a calm, yet firm tone in her voice.

"Your father would like you to take the garbage out now. Since you've paused your game already, why don't you go ahead and take care of it? You can go back to your game after you have taken the garbage out."

Son: "Okay, I'll do it now, mom. And I'm sorry, dad…I really didn't hear you when you asked me to take the garbage out the first time."

Dad: "Apology accepted, son. Next time, I'll make sure that I have your full attention before I begin speaking to you."

In this scenario, the mother was able to diffuse a potentially volatile situation by utilizing a strategy she knew would solve the problem between her husband and her son. You may be wondering how she could have known what to do to get the situation under control so quickly. This mother understood her son's strengths and his unique challenges. She knew that his tendency to hyper-focus on activities that he found enjoyable had probably limited his ability to really listen to and comply with his father's request.

In much the same way, you should also take some time to reflect on and assess your child's strengths and areas of difficulty. Try not to rush through this assessment. It may take you several days or weeks to thoroughly observe your child's behavior, so be prepared and be patient. Take as long as you need to list and describe all of the unique characteristics about your child that make him or her so wonderfully special. What is their favorite food? What is their favorite thing to do? Which self-help skill(s) have they recently mastered? What skill(s) do they continue to have difficulty with? You will discover that as you write about your child, you also become more attuned to him or her. You will begin to see that there is more of a balance between their strengths and their areas of difficulty than you'd realized. Knowing your child's strengths will give you a starting point for many of the strategies in this book.

At times, we as parents and caregivers become so focused on our children's areas of difficulty that we forget to recognize and celebrate their successes! Don't be afraid to make a really big deal about even the smallest of successes, because every success is an important one!

Take some time before you read any further to create a synopsis of your child's personal profile. It may take you only a few minutes to complete this, or it may require several days to complete. Either way, take your time and try to enjoy working on it! Use the suggested profile headers below to guide you as you create your own assessment of your child. If your child is old enough to offer insight and suggestions, allow him to provide as much input as possible during this process.

Suggested profile headers

Likes	Personality traits
Dislikes	Habits
Strengths	Triggers for difficult behaviors
Areas of difficulty	Fears
Dreams and aspirations	Hobbies

Note: You can use the suggested profile headers or you can create your own. To maximize effectiveness, you should try to come up with at least 3-5 items for each area of assessment. You can elaborate on each item as little or as much as you'd like. The goal is to create an accurate "snap shot" of your child which takes his whole person into consideration, not just his areas of difficulty.

Cool Things To Know About

____

(Insert your child's name here)

Nickname: _______________________________

Greatest accomplishment: _________________________________

Favorite thing to do: ______________________________

Favorite food: __________________________________

I.   What does your child like to do?

      a. _______________________________

      b. _______________________________

      c. _______________________________

II.   What are your child's favorite foods?

      a. _______________________________

      b. _______________________________

      c. _______________________________

      d. _______________________________

III.   What is your child really good at?

      a. _______________________________

      b. _______________________________

      c. _______________________________

IV.   What are your child's recent accomplishments?

    a. ____

    b. ____

    c. ____

V.   What does your child dislike the most?

    a. ____

    b. ____

    c. ____

    d. ____

VI.   What does your child have difficulty with?

    a. ____

    b. ____

    c. ____

    d. ____

    e. ____

    f. ____

VII.   What does your child want most?

    a. ____

    b. ____

    c. ____

    d. ____

Note: You can use "Goals and dreams" as one of your assessment areas, even if your child is too young to have his own. Simply write down the goals and dreams that *you* have for your child. Remember that there really is no right or wrong way to do this exercise. However, it will be most meaningful when you take your time to really talk to your child and interact with him before compiling your information.

Chapter Two: Get Organized!

"But even the very hairs of your head are all numbered. Fear not therefore: ye are of more value than many sparrows" Luke 12:7 (KJV)

It's hard to imagine that God, the creator of all things, knows each of us so intimately that he's numbered the hairs on each of our heads! Now that's what I call organized! God cares deeply for us, so He's made it His business to know all there is to know *about* us. In much the same way, as parents, we must learn all that we can about our children so that we can know *them* as intimately as possible.

Once you have really gotten to know your child, it is wise to begin organizing the information that you've gathered. If your child has been diagnosed with a specific type of physical, mental or emotional challenge, it's likely that he or she has at least one doctor or therapist whom he or she sees on a regular basis. In fact, it isn't uncommon for children who are diagnosed with specific challenges to be treated by several medical professionals at once. When my daughter was much younger, she was followed by a neurologist, a geneticist, a psychologist, a physical therapist, a speech therapist, an allergist, a dermatologist, a gastroenterologist, and a general pediatrician – all at the same time!

Your role as a parent takes on new meaning when you begin caring for a differently-abled child. You find yourself being thrust into unfamiliar situations, with little or no time to prepare for or respond to them. This experience can be disorienting and extremely stressful. Getting organized will help you to regain a sense of confidence and peace. My experience has been that it is best to begin keeping copies of your child's medical records right away to ensure that your records are as comprehensive as possible.

The benefits of having copies of your child's medical records may outweigh any difficulties or costs that you incur while trying to obtain them. If your child has several providers working with him at one time, it can be very difficult to keep all of them on the same page! Your child's providers will appreciate your being able to provide them with copies of any relevant notes or letters from other physicians. Having all necessary information in hand will help each physician to gain a more comprehensive understanding of your child's medical history and/or his current medical status, right from the beginning. Physicians may be able to make more timely treatment decisions when they do not have to wait for notes or reports to be sent to them from other physicians. However, the most important benefits of being organized may be to you, the parent. Having your child's records available to you in an organized and easily accessible location will help you to stay on top of everything that is currently going on with your child, as well as any challenges that he may have had in the past. Organized record-keeping will help you as you prepare for doctor's visits or meetings with school personnel.

Getting started may seem overwhelming, especially if you're not really all that organized yourself, but my simple approach to getting organized will have you ready in no time!

Supplies
Two 2.5" or 3" loose leaf binders
A three-hole punch
2 packs of tabbed, loose leaf dividers

That's it! Now you are ready to begin.

I don't recommend that you randomly call each of your child's providers to ask for old records, as many physician's offices have outsourced this service and are almost sure to charge you for it. The exception is, of course, a physician who is no longer treating your child. In this case, you will need to contact the office to let them know that you would like to be sent a copy of your child's records. It is likely you will be charged a fee for this service, so be prepared. If you decide that the associated cost of obtaining the medical records is too great, you shouldn't feel obligated to spend the money to get them. The goal isn't necessarily to obtain a copy of *every* medical record of your child that exists. **Your primary goal is to create a detailed, personal record of your child's treatment history and current medical status, so that you are as informed as possible about his condition.**

Once you have obtained your supplies, begin your quest to become organized during your child's next office visit. Once the doctor has completed her examination, let her know that you would like to have a copy of her office note for your records after it is dictated and placed into your child's medical file. Most doctors don't object to this, but they may suggest that you request the note from their front office personnel. Be sure to request a copy of the office note again when you are checking out or scheduling your child's next appointment.

Over time, you will begin to accumulate valuable information about your child's condition and the care that he is receiving. Use the loose leaf dividers to organize this information as you put it into your binders. How you choose to organize the information is completely up to you. I found it helpful to divide my daughter's information by medical specialty.

For example, all of her neurology records were kept in a section that was labeled "Neurology". All of the information that I received from her geneticist was placed in the section of the binder labeled "Genetics". As time goes on, you may need to purchase more binders. I now have five binders for my daughter, and all of them are chuck full of valuable information on her medical and educational history.

If your child has an IEP (Individualized Educational Plan) or a 504 Plan, your second binder should be used to keep all of your child's IEPs and other school- related information organized. It is vitally important that you know what your child's IEP goals are. You should also know which services and supports school personnel are legally bound to provide to your child, as outlined in his IEP. Having your child's IEPs neatly organized will help you to keep track of this and other important information concerning your child's progress toward his goals. With an organized binder, you will be able to quickly refer to it to find information on your child's PLOP (Present Level of Performance), goals, accommodations, etc. I have often used the information in my daughter's educational binder to support ideas and requests that I've presented to IEP and Child Study teams in meetings at her school. The incorporation of factual and relevant data from my daughter's medical and school records has helped me to present a comprehensive parental statement about my daughter to school IEP teams over the years. Just before the start of every meeting, I would hand each person in attendance a copy of my parental statement. I'd ask everyone to take a few minutes to read the statement before any discussion began, to ensure that everyone involved in the decision-making process concerning my daughter had a good understanding of who she was as a whole person, and not only as a student attending their school.

 School personnel were always impressed with my organization and professionalism in our meetings. In fact, over the years, a few meeting attendees shared with me how much they appreciated the thoroughness and professionalism of my contributions to our discussions, because it helped them to understand my daughter better and to see her in a different light. School systems aren't obligated to give our children the best educational services or placements, but they are required to provide them with educational placements that are *appropriate* for them. Never underestimate the value of presenting yourself in a calm, organized and professional manner when interacting with school personnel. Presenting yourself in this way won't necessarily make it easy for you to get the rest of the team to agree to a service or accommodation you're requesting for your child, but it *will* go a long way toward helping the rest of the group to see you as a competent member of the team whose thoughts and opinions are worth listening to.

Note: Public schools in most states do not charge parents a fee to obtain a copy of their child's school record. Check with your State Board of Education to find out if this is true of the public schools in your area.

Chapter Three: Whose Homework Is It Anyway?

"Peace I leave with you, my peace I give unto you: not as the world giveth, give I unto you. Let not your heart be troubled, neither let it be afraid"
John 14:27 (KJV)

I would be a very rich woman by now if I had a dollar for every time that I've asked myself this very question! So, whose homework is it? The obvious answer is that the homework our children bring home is, in fact, *their* homework. However, as many of you know, children with unique learning styles and needs often require some degree of assistance with their homework assignments. A popular tutoring center is currently running a television commercial on one of our local stations. In it, a young boy approaches his mother and asks for help with his math homework. Without a word and with a panicked expression on her face, his mother turns and runs away! Her son chases right behind her as she runs through their neighborhood, all the while shouting that he needs help with his homework. The mother finally stops running when she reaches the tutoring center and points her son in the direction of a tutor who is standing nearby, ready to help him. I laughed until I cried the first time that I saw this commercial because I could identify with that mother! I've often felt like running away from the agonizing homework struggles that my daughter and I have found ourselves engaged in every evening. Looking back, I suppose that I, too, have "run away" a time or two! I'm not ashamed to say that, on occasion, I've locked myself in my bedroom and asked my daughter to give me about ten minutes to myself, so that I could use that time to pray, cry, do a few deep breathing exercises or just lie down quietly before continuing to help with her homework.

Oh yes, and there was also the time that my husband came home early from his part-time, evening job to find my daughter and me at our wits end! I don't think he'd hung up his coat before I announced that I "needed to get away for awhile" and handed him my daughter's language textbook, advising them both to see what they could figure out together while I was gone! I went to a nearby drug store and aimlessly walked the aisles for about 30 minutes. A half hour may not seem like a long time to you, but it was just long enough for me to settle my thoughts and feelings, regroup and refocus my energy. As I drove home, I prayed and asked God to give me the wisdom and the strength to continue to help my daughter. I also asked Him to continue to help my husband and I to make the right decisions concerning her education. God is still answering these prayers with the passing of each new day and we are very grateful.

Parents who find themselves cast in the role of teacher or tutor night after night will also find that they are faced with some very difficult questions. "Is it possible for me to help *too* much?" or "How do I know she's really struggling with this assignment and not just asking for my help so that she can finish up more quickly?". These are just two examples of the many questions that you may have asked yourself, time and time again. These questions, and others like them, do not have simple answers. The truth is that every child is different, and because they are all wonderfully unique, so are their needs.

There are, however, common characteristics, traits, behaviors and symptoms that many children with learning challenges often possess. While attempting to diagnose their patients, physicians look for these signs as they perform thorough physical examinations and obtain detailed medical histories and other reports from family members, teachers, and school personnel.

After the physician has examined your child and gathered enough data, he or she will likely dictate an office note, detailing the specifics of your child's office visit. This note will often include a diagnosis for your child, assuming that the physician has been able to make one. If you request a copy of the physician's note, you may be able to use it to do a little research of your own on your child's condition. Your research will likely yield valuable information and suggestions - perhaps even a listing of common characteristics or behaviors of people who have that particular condition. For example, while all children with a diagnosis of ADHD are unique, it is likely that many will share certain behavioral characteristics that are common to most people with that particular challenge. Be aware, however, that while the internet is a great tool, you should not allow the information obtained there be the sole measure of your child's ability. Every child is different, even when he or she shares the same diagnosis as other children. It's also important to remember that your child's condition should not be the sole defining trait or characteristic about him. What does the Word of God tell you about who your child is? Let that Word be an integral part of your confession concerning your child.

A thorough physician should be able to provide you with detailed information on your child's condition. This information will be both relevant and helpful to you as you seek to empower your child academically. If you know and understand your child's specific challenges, you will be able to make wiser choices about how best to assist him with his homework.

Do you remember the scenario from Chapter One? The mother in the story was able to quickly assess the situation to help her husband and son avoid an angry confrontation.

She was knowledgeable about her son's tendency to hyper-focus while playing video games and his general difficulties with inattentiveness. She took both factors into consideration when deciding on how to approach him. Your interactions with your child during homework time should be governed in the same way. Use your knowledge of what you know about your child to determine how you interact with him. How much help you give him and what that help "looks" like, will depend on his age, degree to which his specific learning challenges affect him, his unique learning style, etc.

The remainder of this chapter is devoted to the discussion of common areas of homework difficulty. Before continuing, make sure that you've completed the basic assessment of your child's likes, dislikes, needs, strengths, goals and dreams discussed in Chapter One.

<u>Disorganization</u>

Many children, at some point in their development, may appear to be disorganized. In fact, varying degrees of disorganization are expected at different age levels. However, children who fail to eventually master the skills necessary to become organized will often encounter difficulties in their academic pursuits as they progress through their school years. For example, children who have weak organizational skills may be unable to copy their homework assignments completely and accurately from a chalkboard or white board. They may also have difficulty remembering which textbooks or worksheets to bring home to complete their homework assignments each night.

Their loose leaf binders may be in complete disarray, making it difficult for them to find and keep up with important papers. Their book bags, lockers and living spaces may also be extremely messy.

<u>Forgetfulness</u>

I know. It can be hard to believe and accept that your child really *did* forget the instructions that you gave her just a minute ago! After all, she was looking right at you while you were speaking to her, and she assured you that she'd understood what you were asking of her. How could she not remember the details of a conversation that took place just a few minutes before? It can be equally as difficult to acknowledge that your child has so quickly forgotten the steps to a math problem that the two of you have been working on for the past half hour. Forgetfulness is a trait shared by many children with unique learning styles (and some of us over the age of 40, but we'll save that discussion for a different book!) A short attention span, sensory integration difficulties, inattentiveness or other challenges, can make it very difficult for children with memory challenges to remember even simple, recent events or instructions. For some children, even daily, routine personal hygiene tasks are easily forgotten if they are not prompted to perform them.

<u>Lack of Confidence / Learned Helplessness</u>

Knowing just how much help to give with homework is, perhaps, the one question that many parents struggle with most. As previously stated, several factors come into play when trying to make decisions about how to best assist your child with homework. If your child has been diagnosed with a specific condition or learning challenge, you may already know which areas he will need the most help in. But should the presence of a specific area of difficulty be the sole determining factor that dictates how you help your child? Well-meaning parents sometimes offer *too* much help to their children, in the interest of helping them to obtain good grades or to prevent them from having homework meltdowns. Many parents don't realize that helping too much now could actually adversely affect their child's level of independence later in life. Still, knowing when your child *really* needs help versus when he is asking for help because he's given up and doesn't want to put in the effort required to complete his homework, can be a very difficult call. You won't always make the right decisions, but having done your own "homework" concerning your child and his unique learning style should at least give you the assurance of knowing that your decisions are intelligent and informed ones.

<u>Sensory and Fine Motor Difficulties</u>

Although seemingly unlikely culprits, sensory and fine motor difficulties can also contribute to your child's homework struggles. For example, some children may not be comfortable with the "feel" of a pencil in their hand when they are writing. Other children may have preferences about which types of pens they use because they are uncomfortable with the way that certain pens "feel" when they are writing with them. I, personally, prefer the "feel" of a ball point pen when writing (as opposed to that of a fine point pen) because my hand movements seem smoother and more fluid when I write with a ball point pen. I don't like the "feel" of writing with a pencil at all (sort of feels like I'm dragging my nails down a chalkboard) because of the friction caused by the pencil point meeting the surface that I'm writing on. Unlike me, my daughter actually prefers to write with a fine point pen. She feels as though she has more control over this type of pen and that her handwriting is neater when she uses one. Improper lighting can also have an undesirable effect on a child's ability to focus and concentrate on homework assignments. Lights that are too bright may cause a glare on notebook or textbook pages, forcing a child to strain to read the text. Conversely, lights that are too dim will also force a child to strain to read the text. Either way, improper lighting can be a significant distraction to a child trying to complete homework.

A barking dog, a loud television, and even family members engaged in an ongoing conversation have the potential to over stimulate a child's sensory system as well, preventing her from being able to concentrate fully on her homework.

Fatigue

On school days, most school-aged children wake up very early in the morning. Unlike babies or toddlers, they are not given an opportunity to nap during the day, making the average school day very long and tiring for them. A child with ongoing, night-time sleep difficulties may be even more exhausted by the end of a typical school day. Children who attend afterschool programs until the early evening hours have an extremely long day to contend with as well. It's no wonder that many children are often exhausted by the time they arrive at home each evening. This mental, emotional, sensory and physical fatigue can adversely affect a child's ability to focus on his homework. Increased levels of fatigue may also inhibit his ability to regulate his emotions. His frustration tolerance is likely to be quite low, often contributing to a display of undesirable behaviors.

Now that we've identified some contributing factors for homework difficulties, it's time to talk about solutions! Remember that if your child is experiencing ongoing academic difficulties, it is vitally important that you consider having professional educational and psychological evaluations performed to identify or rule out the presence of specific learning, neurological or psychological disorders.

Perhaps you have been reluctant to have this kind of testing performed for your child. To fully understand and support your child, it is imperative that you are armed with as much information about him as possible. The appropriate testing may provide you with much of the information that you will need. Having your own, independent evaluations performed will also give you data to compare to that of your child's school, should such testing ever be recommended and performed by school personnel.

Note: As a parent or caregiver, there are probably several more areas of concern or other problem behaviors (specific to your child), that you would add to this list of potential homework distractions. Be sure to write them all down so that you will be able to easily identify them as you see them occurring. Writing them down will give you a starting point for your plan of action. Developing a plan of action that is right for you and your child will be discussed in a later chapter.

Chapter Four: Assembling the Pieces

In the remaining chapters of the book, we'll discuss specific strategies to help you and your child get through daily homework assignments. Before endeavoring to assist your child with his or her homework, you must understand that your child is a wonderfully complex and unique individual. Complete with a physical body, emotions, thoughts and perceptions, it's likely that your child still sees most issues from his or her own perspective. In fact, the ability to see and understand the perspectives of others is a skill that many children have difficulty with at some point in their development. That being said, it will be important to pack a few extra doses of patience in your bag of tricks as you embark on this new journey!

It can be very difficult to know when our children genuinely need help with their homework. It can be even more difficult to know *how much* help to offer. Over a period of time, a pattern has emerged with my daughter's behavior which has helped us to better understand her needs and answer these questions. By listening to and classifying the types of questions she asks us and by asking her teachers for their feedback and opinions, we've been able to establish a list of skills and concepts that we know she will probably find the most challenging. Being armed with this valuable information, however, isn't always enough to help us determine if her requests for help are genuine. We've learned that it is often best to at least consider that she may actually need help with some of her homework rather than refuse to help her based on our assumptions about what we think that she should already know or remember.

We begin by encouraging her to use the information that she *does* understand to try to figure out the answer to the problem at hand on her own. Utilizing this approach helps to minimize learned dependency, while boosting her self-confidence at the same time. Your child may also have a difficult time remembering the steps to complete some of her homework assignments, even after you've gone over them with her. Difficulties with retention and organization can make it difficult for children to memorize facts and concepts in several subject areas. Understanding how their unique learning styles impact their ability to complete homework assignments on their own will help you to set realistic goals and expectations for them.

Helping children to organize the information that they already have about a problem or task is often enough to get them off to a good start!

When children become frustrated, they can have a difficult time sorting through their emotions. As a result, they may be unable to tell us exactly what they need help with during homework time. At the peak of their frustration, they may not be able to offer detailed verbal explanations of the problems that they are experiencing and may find it easier to cry, whine or become defiant. Your child's frustration may be stemming from the fact that he's just realized that he didn't write down the correct homework assignment and now, can't seem to figure out what he should be doing. Or, perhaps, he's become frustrated because he simply can't remember the explanations and examples that the teacher gave in class. To make matters worse, he can't find the piece of loose-leaf paper that he used to take notes.

The possibilities of what could be wrong are many, so you'll have to be a keen listener and an even better observer to help your child navigate an emotional crisis. It is up to you to patiently work with your child to find out exactly where his difficulties lie. What should the help that we provide to our children be like? Is there a "one size fits all" model for offering homework assistance? Every child is unique, and *because* each child is so unique, effective interventions of any kind should be personalized and specific to each child's needs and strengths.

Learned dependency is a very real concern for children with learning differences. Our daughter, like many other children, would like nothing more than for us to hold her hand and guide her through each one of her homework assignments, every night of the week! Our desire to help her to become as independent as possible is what keeps us going as we encourage her to independently complete as much of her homework as she can. Homework help can take on many forms. Each family's unique set of circumstances will help to dictate what this help involves for their children. At our house, for example, help with homework is sometimes as simple as reminding our daughter to stick to her evening homework schedule to make staying on task easier.

A schedule assigns a specific length of time to each task or activity that is listed, helping to solidify the concept of passing time.

Assistance with homework can also be offered by making positive, encouraging statements to your child about what you believe he can accomplish. When your child is upset, your acknowledgement of his frustration can go a long way toward "disarming" him and helping him to see that you really do understand what he is going through. Once this acknowledgement has been made, your child may be more willing to listen to other things that you may have to say.

I often use language like this when speaking to my own daughter. For example, speaking in a firm, yet loving tone I might say "I know this isn't easy for you, but I also know that you'll give it your best shot. I'm so proud of you for at least trying." Leaving her alone to process what I've said and make her own decision about whether or not she is willing to try again are sometimes enough to get her over a homework hurdle. At times, however, it is necessary for me to actually sit down beside her and patiently offer guidance and support as she works through a problem or assignment that is particularly troublesome for her. There is no guarantee that a particular solution will fit every homework hurdle every time, so flexibility and creativity on your part will be extremely important.

Remember the thoughts and emotions that I mentioned a few paragraphs back? Your child's thoughts and emotions are just two of the many variables that will influence his or her ability to complete homework. A child who is sick, anxious, angry or depressed may become distracted by her own thoughts and feelings, making it difficult for her to focus on completing her homework assignments.

It is important, then, for parents to pay attention to their child's nonverbal behavior and factor in the possibility that any extremes in behavior could be an indication that something is wrong. Children often lack insight into their own behavior and may not be able to understand why they're behaving a certain way, nor will they be able to articulate this to you. Listening to and observing your child will help you to better understand what's on his mind. Try to keep an open mind about what might be distracting your child or causing him anxiety. It's not uncommon for a child's memory of a distressing event that has occurred earlier, either the same day or further back in the past, to suddenly resurface and cause the child a tremendous amount of anxiety.

So, where should you begin in your quest to help your child? Acknowledging any negative feelings or anxieties that *you* may be harboring about your child's homework difficulties is a great place to start!

Be honest with yourself about how you feel because only then can you be honest with yourself, and others, about what you need.

There will be days that you feel energized, optimistic and ready to assist your child. There will also be days that you just want to curl up into a ball and cry because you're mentally and emotionally exhausted *from* helping your child. It's okay to feel either of these emotions or any combination of emotion(s) that might fall in between. Allow yourself to be a thinking, feeling human being. While you're at it, forgive yourself for not being that super hero that you'd convinced yourself you had to be when you realized that your child was differently-abled. God is responsible for the miraculous in our lives. As parents, our job is simply to believe His Word and trust Him with our children and our hearts.

Raising a child with unique challenges is no easy task. Remember to carve out a little time for yourself each day to do something that you enjoy. If possible, try to do something during this time period that doesn't involve your child so that your focus will remain on you! I often find my "me time" on Saturday mornings while the rest of my family sleeps in. How I love the peace and quiet that fill the early morning hours! I'm able to pray, think, plan, worship, or anything else that I want to do during this time because I'm all alone. I have found that I am at my best when I maintain realistic expectations of how I will respond to the challenges that each day brings.

I try to take life one day at a time, being careful not to get ahead of God's plan for me or my family. I could go on and on about the importance of taking time to rejuvenate yourself, but I'll have to save the rest of that "sermon" for another time. What's important now, is for us to get back to discussing ways to create a daily homework routine for you and your child that works!

I. Allow time for reflection: I suggest that you begin each afternoon or evening with your child by asking her about her day. Children won't always volunteer information about events or people that have upset them, so it's a good idea to ask questions like, "Did you have a good day today?" "Did anything exciting happen?" "Who did you play with during recess?" or "Did anything happen today that made you feel sad or afraid?" Encouraging your child talk about her feelings may help to "clear the air" and set the stage for a more tranquil homework period. This period of bonding with your child can double as a period of transition. Many children have difficulty transitioning from one place or activity to another.

The transition from school or an afterschool program is no exception. Offer your child a healthy snack and the opportunity to settle down before asking her to begin her homework.

II. Use a schedule: Unstructured time may be a major source of stress and anxiety for your child. Prior to implementing an effective homework plan, it may help if you take time to create a realistic homework schedule for your child to follow first. Make sure that the schedule includes breaks at regular intervals. The subject order, length of work and break times, and any other entries must be arranged with your child's uniqueness in mind. For example, the incorporation of three, 10 minute breaks into one child's schedule may work beautifully, while another child will get much more accomplished without displaying any difficult behaviors with just two, 15 minute breaks instead. A sample of my daughter's current homework/evening schedule is below.

<u>Evening Schedule</u>

5:30 - 5:45PM	**Arrive at home; Break**
5:45 - 6:00PM	**Study Bible verse, spelling and vocabulary words**
6:00 - 6:30PM	**Complete unfinished homework**
6:30 - 6:45PM	**BREAK**
6:45 - 7:00PM	**Study bolded textbook terms for science and history**
7:00 - 7:30PM	**DINNER**

7:30 - 8:15PM	**Complete unfinished homework** **Read (15 minutes)**
8:15 - 8:30PM	**Bath/shower; Brush teeth**
8:30 - 9:00PM	**Free time if all homework is** **complete**
9:00 - 9:15PM	**Good night! Lights out!**

The use of schedules can be tricky with children who are very literal or extremely rigid in their thought and behavior patterns. Extreme emotional reactions or tantrums may result when even slight deviations from their schedules become necessary. You know your child best. If a written schedule has the potential to become more of a hindrance than a help to her, you may want to explore other ways of establishing a basic level of consistency during her homework and study periods.

III. Minimize distractions: Provide your child with a "homework zone" that is as free from distractions as possible. Remember that there may be very specific noises, movements, temperatures, etc. that you child finds distracting. Take these into consideration when planning and preparing an area for your child to complete homework. My daughter once insisted that doing her homework in front of the television with her favorite show on was best because the television "helped her to concentrate." I chuckled to myself a bit while she continued in her attempts to persuade me to allow the television to remain on during homework time. "The T.V. relaxes me. Don't you want me to be relaxed when I'm doing my homework?" she asked sweetly. Impressed with the calm, rational way in which she'd made her case, I surprised us both when I agreed to allow the television to remain on while she completed her math homework. My strategy was to allow the television to stay on so she could see for herself that the television was, indeed, a huge distraction for her.   In the end, as I suspected would be the case, she was unable to focus on her work enough to complete the assignment with the television on. I was sure that she would realize and acknowledge that this was the case, but she didn't!   Surprisingly, she argued that she hadn't finished her assignment because she was tired, not because she'd been distracted. Remember that lack of insight that I mentioned earlier? This was a perfect example of it, right here! Nevertheless, I explained that I'd been fair about letting her try things her way, and since she hadn't completed her assignment, she would now have to turn the television off. It was her turn to be fair by trying things my way, I reminded her. She pondered this for a few seconds and then replied "Okay, mommy. I'll turn it off". The question of having the television on during homework time has never come up again!

Chapter 5: Ready or Not!

What kinds of mental images does the word sacrifice conjure up for you? For me, visions of myself sweating as I work hard to ensure the success or safety of another person, readily pop into my mind. I also imagine Jesus as He hung dying on the cross; not because of anything that He'd done but, rather, to pay the price for the sins of all mankind.

The journey that you've found yourself on with your child has already, undoubtedly, required you to make a few adjustments and sacrifices in your life. Perhaps you've had to forego a cherished night out with your friends more often than you would have liked to. Or maybe your church hasn't been as welcoming or accommodating of your child as you thought they would be. Whatever your situation, I'm fairly certain that you've had to make adjustments in some area of your life since you began this journey.

It was necessary for me to leave my job in the corporate environment for six years after my daughter was born to make sure that she received the therapies and interventions that would help her. My faith in God's ability to continue to provide for our family was strong, so I really didn't worry much about our finances. However, because there was significantly less money coming into our household, my family had to make major lifestyle changes in order to survive financially. We were a family of five (eight if you counted our pet dog and guinea pigs!) with many bills and other financial obligations which still had to be met. When I reflect on this time in our lives, I am reminded of the perfect and complete way that God provided for our family.

It was no coincidence that during this time, I was introduced to a woman who housed a community food pantry at her home. She needed a volunteer to take over the Tuesday food pick up from a local grocery store. "You can take first pick of whatever you pick up, and just bring the rest here to help keep the pantry stocked", she'd said. Grateful, and equally amazed, I agreed to take on the job. As it turns out, God used that once-per-week, volunteer food pick up to feed our family for almost two years! I found it interesting that it rained on at least half of those Tuesdays. I don't like driving in the rain, but I smiled inside each time that it rained on a Tuesday back then because to me, the rain symbolized the showers of blessing that the Lord was faithfully pouring into our lives. He'd told me that He would be glorified, even in our struggles, and He was making good on His Word to us!

Then, there was the homemade cookie "business" that was started with just the pennies from an old coffee jar! Now, this wasn't actually a real business. I'd made cookies for a few of our friends and my husband's coworkers one Christmas, and to my surprise everyone absolutely loved them! I had never made cookies from scratch, so you can imagine my surprise when people began to ask if they could place orders for more! I decided to take a leap of faith to find out what God was up to. I had no extra money to purchase the ingredients that I would need to bake a large amount of cookies, so I rolled up all of the pennies that I'd saved over the past several months in an old coffee jar. When I was finished, I had rolled up a total of $11 in pennies. I took the pennies to my bank and exchanged them for paper currency. After a quick trip to the local grocery store for baking ingredients, I was ready to get started! The rest of the story is nothing short of a miracle. In no time, I was having a difficult time keeping up with the demand for cookies!

Some people were able to pay for my sweet treats, while others could not. I baked cookies day in and day out to fill orders for both my paying and non-paying customers. Money was tight for us back then, but this really didn't matter much to me. I was just happy to be doing something that made other people happy! Not only had I finally found something to do that allowed me to focus on things that had nothing to do with doctors or therapists, I'd also found a way to be a blessing to other people. I wanted my cookies to make people smile the way that I had, several years before, when my mother brought me cookies during a particularly rough time in my life. At twelve days old, our oldest daughter was recovering in the hospital from emergency open-heart surgery. I was feeling a tidal wave of different emotions and, consequently, having a hard time getting my bearings again. As I sat at my newborn baby's bedside, I was shocked, confused, and afraid. "Just a little something to keep you sweet", mom said as she'd entered the room and handed me the cookies. I've never forgotten her words that day or the wonderful way that receiving such a simple gift had made me feel! The sweet simplicity of my mother's gift reminded me of God's pure and unfailing love toward us at a time when I'd needed that reminder most.

After several weeks, I'd perfected my recipe for five different types of cookies. A local store owner even offered to stock my cookies in his store and sell them to his customers! I graciously declined his offer, but was flattered nonetheless! Yes, God is truly amazing. The small monetary donations that people gave to us for their cookies were a tremendous help to our family. The miraculous had occurred in a seemingly bleak and hopeless situation! In the Bible, Jesus multiplied the fish and the loaves to feed thousands of hungry people. In our home, He'd multiplied the seemingly small pocket change from an old coffee jar and the gifts that people gave to us to accomplish the impossible too!

You may be wondering how this story is even remotely relevant to the concept of sacrifice. I'd had a good job when our youngest daughter was born. My husband also had a good job, so our bills were current and always paid on time. We'd even managed to begin putting a little money away for retirement, emergencies and the like. Making the decision to stop working indefinitely so that our daughter could receive the early intervention services that she needed wasn't a hard one to make, but I knew that our lives would be very different because of it. As the parent of a differently-abled child, you may find yourself facing a similar decision. Large or small, there will be sacrifices to make along the way in your quest to ensure that your child is healthy, happy, appreciated and loved. Searching for the right balance while managing your own needs and the needs of your child and other family members, will likely be an ongoing effort, but one that you must continually seek to establish. A daunting task, indeed, even for the most vigilant super mom or dad! Still, despite the enormity of the challenge, your efforts should yield very positive and lasting results if you are consistent.

Let's talk for a moment about the concept of acceptance. Do you know what it means to truly accept something or someone?

True acceptance occurs when one wholeheartedly believes that information received about another person, place or thing is unequivocally true.

When chronic illness or other long-term circumstances come into our lives, it's a good idea to occasionally "step back" from those circumstances to assess our positioning and our approach to them. As Christians, our belief and hope should be that God loves us and wants what's best for us and our families.

This is a fundamental belief that you must have in order to take a firm stand with your faith to believe God for His best concerning your child and your family. Did you know that the Bible says that Christians will have difficulties (just like everyone else) in their lives? The blessed assurance that we have, however, is that God is right there by our side, rooting for us and doing all that He can to work our circumstances out for our good.

Living with difficult circumstances for prolonged periods of time can be difficult. Establishing a balance is critical under these types of conditions. For me, this balance is achieved daily and is part of a process that I call "hide and seek". I realize that this may sound a bit odd to you, but please hear me out! My version of hide and seek begins with the purposeful defining and classifying of the circumstances into two categories - those that I will only acknowledge and those that I will both acknowledge *and* accept. When I acknowledge the presence of a difficult circumstance in my life, I allow it to occupy just a little of my mental, emotional and spiritual "space", simply because it is a part of my reality at that time. In a very basic and natural sense, there are many ills and other problems that can befall any one of us at any given time. This, my friend, is a part of our human existence.

Acknowledging that a problem or difficult circumstance exists doesn't mean that you have accept it.

This separation of "things acknowledged" and "things accepted" has changed my life. For example, when my daughter was diagnosed with autism and a significant speech delay at the age of two, I acknowledged that there were concerns with her development.

With the Lord's leading, my husband and I were able to find the right placements, interventions and service providers for her. Our actions were a way of acknowledging our circumstances, but didn't necessarily indicate our acceptance of them. "Hide and seek" for us meant acknowledging the reality of the circumstances, "hiding" or not allowing the unnecessary aspects of those circumstances to impact our lives, and seeking the Lord's guidance and wisdom every step of the way.

Taking this approach has empowered me to effectively deal with the difficulties that often come with raising a uniquely gifted child. Purposefully deciding what I give my attention and energy to has given me a sense of control in seemingly hopeless situations. My family and I are not victims of any situation, person, or event. Instead, we are always victorious because of Christ!

Chapter Six: Do You Hear What I Hear?

"Trust in the Lord with all thine heart; and lean not unto thine own understanding. In all thy ways acknowledge him, and he shall direct thy paths" Proverbs 3:5-6 (KJV)

Employing the "hide and seek principle" for a sustained period of time should help you to develop a more sensitive ear; in both a natural and a spiritual sense. Focusing on what *is* possible instead of what you consider to be impossible, will help to train your "hearing". When your "hearing" is lined up with your faith, you will begin to see possibilities and opportunities that you hadn't seen before. You've got to decide right now what you're going to allow yourself to "hear" and accept as the truth concerning your child.   Don't be afraid to dream and set goals for him. It's okay to acknowledge that your circumstances may have changed the way that you'll need to approach some things right now, but wallowing in sadness, fear and anger won't help the situation one bit! Your time and energy is better spent on being optimistic about your child's future, and putting plans in place to help him achieve his goals and dreams.

As a parent or caregiver, you probably experienced a range of strong emotions when you first received your child's diagnosis. Fear, anger, disappointment and sadness may have been just a few of them. The implications were clear and for a while, perhaps, your confidence and optimism were silenced as fear took over and called your child's purpose and potential into question. "Would he ever walk?" you may have wondered. After all, the doctor had diagnosed him with cerebral palsy, hadn't he? Parent or caregivers of children with intellectual challenges may have found themselves wondering if their child was capable of learning anything at all!

These, and similar concerns, are all reasonable questions to have when you are told that your child has a disability or long-term health problem. However, at some point, *you* will have to decide what the answers to those questions will be. The answers that you accept and believe in your heart will be directly influenced by what I call your "response - ability".

Your "response-ability" is your ability to respond to adversity in ways that are positive, optimistic and meaningful.

If you have great "response-ability", you will continue to dream for your child and set goals for him or her. If your "response-ability" isn't so great, you will likely find it difficult to envision your child being successful at all.

I'm reminded of a time when our daughter was quite young - perhaps two or three years old. I was completely overwhelmed emotionally, and desperate to find other parents whose children had challenges that were similar to those that she had. I joined two local support groups for parents of children with unique challenges. The emotional support that I found in both was refreshing and stabilizing. I learned a lot about my daughter's health conditions, and even found ways to encourage and mentor other parents. I was thankful for both groups and looked forward to the weekly meetings because, for the first time in a long time, I didn't feel completely isolated and alone. After about six months, however, I began to feel the Lord's leading to withdraw from both groups. Initially, I couldn't image that God, after having led me to these support groups, would now be asking me to back away from them. I was sitting at my dining room table reading one afternoon, when I sensed the Lord speaking to me, drawing my focus away from my daughter's challenges and back to Him.

I began to realize that I *had* inadvertently begun to roll my daughter's identity into the challenges and circumstances she was facing at that time in her life. I'd found a great deal of comfort in researching autism and talking to other parents about their children's challenges. In the recesses of my mind, I guess I believed that having an in-depth understanding of autism would help me to stay a step ahead of it. That knowledge, while incredibly empowering, was even more suffocating because I had no idea how to use it. I read every book about autism that I could get my hands on. Reading books and researching autism and developmental disabilities became my subconscious way of trying to tame and subdue my daughter's challenges. It was empowering to feel like I was, once again, in control of what was happening to her. I needed to feel that her challenges and difficulties had not won the war! In retrospect, I now realize that I'd somehow forgotten that it was ultimately God whom I should have been looking to for direction all along instead of myself. With all of the knowledge that I'd amassed, had I ever really been in control anyway?

Even though I didn't fully understand why God was asking it of me, I decided to stop attending the support group meetings, as He had asked. I'm not in any way suggesting that you shouldn't take advantage of support groups. My situation was unique to me, just as yours is unique to you *and only you.* This simply wasn't the path that I was supposed to be on at that time in my life. So if you're involved with a great support group and you have a sense of peace about being there, by all means stick with it!

The information that I'd gathered on autism, sensory integration disorder and speech delay was very helpful for my daughter and my family.

However, God knew that if I didn't adjust my focus soon, I would be consumed by my own preoccupation with these very things, and the struggles that had come along with them. Remember our discussion about acknowledgement versus acceptance in the last chapter? It seems that I'd begun to accept that my daughter would always have difficulty interacting with others, language problems, profound sensory difficulties and seizures. At that time, I didn't have a revelation about how to acknowledge my circumstances without accepting them. As I went about caring for my daughter and preparing her for the future, I'd begun to rely solely on my own ability to find the right information to help her instead of relying on God to lead the way.

When I stopped going to the support groups, some of the other parents wanted to know why. At first, I wasn't really sure what to tell them, so I made up excuses. I told them that I just didn't have the time to attend meetings anymore. Soon, I began to feel convicted about not being completely honest, so I decided to just tell them the truth. "I believe that God is leading me in a different direction now", was my response to the next person who asked. Obviously taken aback, but intrigued, this mother wanted to know more. We talked for another fifteen minutes or so, mainly about our children and our dreams for them. I told her that I knew a lot about what the prognosis was for a child with autism could be, but I knew even more about a God who was bigger than autism or any other diagnosis that my daughter had! It was truly a liberating and freeing moment for us both. Since that day, the Lord has helped us to keep our lives pretty well balanced. Our family has had some really difficult days along the way, but we've learned a lot and are stronger for it, both individually and collectively.

Take a few minutes now to quiet yourself and really think about where your focus is. I'm certain that caring for your child requires a great deal of your emotional, mental and physical energy, and that is perfectly okay! However, starting today, I want you to begin to challenge yourself to find a balance that is right for you and your family. Each new day will bring with it a new set of circumstances - some good, some not so good. Your daily goal is to find ways to create and maintain a sense of peace and balance in your life and in your home. This is important so please, try not to rush through this. Use the sample guide provided on the next page to get started. I suggest using this worksheet in the morning, as you begin each day. This will help to set a positive tone and lay the foundation for a day that is filled with possibility and purpose.

Daily Balance Worksheet

Date: ___________

Word or Prayer of Encouragement: This can be an inspirational quote, a scripture reference, a funny joke or anything that makes you smile or feel good!

____

____

____

Current Stressors: List any and everything that is a cause of stress or anxiety for you today.

____

____

____

Natural Answers and Solutions: List ideas and thoughts that you've come up with to deal with your stressors from a natural perspective.

____

____

____

Spiritual Answers and Solutions: List any answers to prayer, scripture references, song lyrics, etc. that increase your hope and bring you peace.

____

____

____

"You shall go out in joy, and be led
back in peace; the mountains and the
hills before you shall burst into song
and all the trees of the field shall clap
their hands"

Isaiah 55:12(KJV)

Chapter Seven: The Ten R's of Reacting (Or Not!)

There's an old saying that says we should "choose our battles wisely". I've always understood this to mean that I should take time to assess any difficult situation that I find myself in and try to make a sound, intelligent decision about how (or if) I will expend valuable time and energy trying to resolve it. I've utilized this strategy many times, often with pleasing results. Out of all the areas in my life, however, I've found that employing this strategy has proven to be most difficult in my "battles" with my own children. At some point, most children will inevitably disappoint shock or infuriate their parents when they behave in a manner that is disrespectful, defiant or rebellious. Is it because our egos are bruised when we have to admit that our little angels aren't quite as angelic as we thought they were? Still worse, could their (hopefully temporary) outlandish behavior have been caused by our now seemingly ineffective parenting skills?

When children exhibit difficult behaviors, there are a number of very important factors that must be considered.

You must recognize and accept that your child uses behavior as a means of communication. This is often a subconscious means of communicating on their part, but the behavior carries a message nonetheless. All behavior means something!

As parents and caregivers, part of our job is to find out what the messages in those difficult behaviors are. Use the strategies on the next page to help you navigate your child's emotional outbursts. When he regains control of himself, try to help him understand all that has happened and be willing to let go of your own frustration so that you both can move on.

<u>The Ten R's of Reacting (Or Not!)</u>

1. Recognize - that your child is probably less capable of using an acceptable means of communicating when he is frustrated or upset. He may need your help to restore order to his thoughts and behavior. Be willing to help him organize the chain of events that led to the current crisis.

2. Realize - that your child's emotions are in control when he is upset and that his attempts at self-control and self-regulation may fail initially. Be patient. This too shall pass!

3. Respect - the fact that his emotions are real. Show empathy by telling your child that you understand that he is having a hard time. Your verbal acknowledgement of his feelings may help to calm him. Try not to speak too much, however, as excessive talking may further agitate your child.

4. Remember - that it can be more difficult for him to "keep the problem small" and take the perspectives of other people when he is upset. He may also have difficulty responding to others with the appropriate level of emotion, so be prepared for loud, dramatic and possibly inappropriate outbursts and responses. Try not to overreact to your child's out of control behavior. Choose your battles wisely!

5. Regulate - the duration of his emotional outbursts. Set a specific, yet realistic time limit and let your child know that when the specified amount of time has almost passed, he will be expected to begin trying to "put the problem behind him" and move on to more productive and acceptable behavior.

6.   Re-state - the problem for your child when he is calm enough to listen to you speak. Use clear, concise language, with as few words as possible. Offer honest answers to his questions about the problem and the events that led up to it.

7.   Remove - yourself from your child's space to give him the privacy, time and opportunity necessary to cycle through his emotions in his attempt to regain his composure on his own and in his own way. It is important that your child learns how to independently take the steps necessary to calm himself and move on.

8.   Responsibility - remind your child that he must always take responsibility for his own actions and behavior. If your child caused any harm or damage to anyone or anything while he was upset, you must help him to understand the natural consequences of his own behavior. Wait until he is completely calm before attempting to have this dialogue with him, as discussing consequences prematurely will almost always lead to subsequent tantrums or meltdowns.

9.   Remind - your child to apologize to those who may have been impacted by his difficult behavior. It is best to wait until your child has completely calmed down before trying to initiate this kind of dialogue as well.

10. Regroup - help your child to transition back to his homework or to a new activity. Remember that your child has experienced very strong emotions and may require a significant amount of time to calm down before he can successfully move on in a new direction.

These suggested interventions may not work for every situation, but they do offer common-sense strategies that should help to diffuse many of your child's emotionally charged outbursts. Complete the Emotion Diary on the next few pages with your child at a time when he is calm and in a relatively good mood. Knowing his emotional triggers ahead of time may help you to respond to him more appropriately during a crisis.

<u>My Emotion Diary</u>

Read and think about the name of the emotion in each statement below.
Write a response on the line provided and circle any additional answers that
apply.

1. **I feel afraid when** _______________________________

I am at school	I take tests or quizzes
I am on the school bus	I am in the school cafeteria
I am in my bed at night	I am in the mall
I am in a movie theater	I am in a grocery store
I am at the doctor's office	I am at the dentist's office

My teacher asks me a question

I am alone	Strangers are near
I am at school	Riding in a car
I am near dogs	I hear loud noises

I am around large groups of people

Crossing busy streets	Asked to try new things

Asked to let others know how I really feel

2. **I feel sad when** _______________________________

I don't understand my school work

Someone yells at me	Others laugh at me
I am bored	Others ignore me
Others don't feel well	I don't feel well
I am at home	I am at school
I am alone	I am with others
No one likes me	All of the time

No one understands me

I wake up in the morning	I am in class

I'm at my daycare or after-school program

I forget things	I lose things
I have to do chores	My parents leave for work

I don't understand other kid's jokes

I don't do well on tests or quizzes

3. **I feel angry when** _______________________________

I don't understand what others are saying

I don't understand my school work

People tease me   I don't get my way

No one will help me   No one believes me

I am asked to do something that I don't want to do

Someone that I love is sick

Someone that I love has died

I don't know how to do my homework

No one listens to me   Someone hits me

Someone yells at me   I am ignored

I feel different from everyone else

It is time to begin my homework

All the time   Plans change suddenly

I get home from school or daycare

4. **I feel happy when** _________________________________

I am at home   I am at school

I am at a friend's house   I am at church

I remember that I am unique and special

I remember that my family loves me   I am eating

I am at the mall   I am doing homework

I think about my friends

I get everything that I ask for

My teacher asks me a question in class

I go to bed at night   I am in the grocery store

I am talking   Others are talking

I do well on tests and quizzes

I get an allowance for completing my chores

I am reading   School is out

I'm asked to write about my feelings

Parenting a differently-abled child can be quite challenging at times. Each new day brings with it the possibility of new challenges, (as well as many of the same challenges from the day before) so hang in there! Each new day will also usher in the sweetness and the mercy of God, so don't forget to make prayer a part of your daily routine. As parents and caregivers, our patience may wear thin and we may feel as if our faith is hanging on by just a thread, but remember that you are not alone!

"Let us therefore come boldly unto the throne of grace, that we may obtain mercy, and find grace to help in time of need"
Hebrews 4:16

Despite these and other challenges, it *is* possible for you and your family to have the peace and direction of God in every situation that you face. God wants the very best for you and your family! You must be clear on this before you can endeavor to apply His word to your lives. If this is a new way of thinking about God and His Will for you, take some time to read your bible and meditate on God's goodness. The book of Psalms might be a good place to start, as many of these scriptures tell of God's goodness and protection.

What, then, is the key to discovering a life of abundance in the midst of such struggle? The answer is balance. Balance must be achieved with the information that your circumstances report to you *and what God has to say about them.* There may be times when the reality of your situation seems contrary to what you believe God is saying about it. Try not to allow yourself to be completely discouraged by what you are able to see, hear and feel or by the difficulties that your child may be experiencing.

You will need to acknowledge the presence of these difficulties, and maybe even act on them, but you should also pray about the situation and ask the Lord for His leading. For me, maintaining balance means that **for every action that I take in the natural to address a particular circumstance, I take two in realm of my faith to ensure that I am attuned to God's leading.** This also helps me to relinquish my fear, anger and hopelessness to God through prayer on a regular basis. After all, it is His job to make provision for our family, not mine!

You must also find a way to balance your thinking. Focusing exclusively on the difficult aspects of your journey will circumvent your prayers and cause you to fall into despair.

The focus of your words, thoughts and feelings will eventually become your reality!

Instead, focus your energy on creating meaningful and pleasant memories with your child. Your cheerfulness and optimism will inspire her to have a more positive outlook. Through your words and actions, you will also be teaching her important lessons about using her faith to trust in God's love and provision for her life. Remind her often that God loves her unconditionally.

Every person is born with purpose. No matter what our circumstances, we **all** have something to contribute to the world. Sharing our purpose with others is a way of realizing our destiny. We enrich our own lives and the lives of others when we unleash the unique gift(s) that God has blessed each one of us with. Commit yourself to helping your child discover his unique, God-given gifts and talents. As you identify these gifts, help your child to nurture them, with the ultimate goal of sharing them with others.

You may need to employ unconventional means to accomplish this, but the end result will be well worth the effort.

"For if the willingness is there, the gift is acceptable according to what one has, not according to what he does not have" 2 Corinthians 8:12 (NIV)

You are well-equipped for this journey. Ask God to help *you* as you help your child to stir up his or her unique gifts and talents. Who knows? You may even unmask some of your own unique gifts and talents along the way!

~~~~~~~~~~~~~~~~~~~~~~

"For I know the plans I have for you," declares the Lord. "Plans to prosper you and not to harm you, Plans to give you hope and a future"

Jeremiah 29:11 (NIV)

~~~~~~~~~~~~~~~~~~~~~~

Appendix A: Sample Letters and Forms

PARENTAL STATEMENT OF CONCERN
SAMPLE LETTER

Date:

Re: (name of child)

Purpose of letter (i.e. request for evaluation or re-evaluation)

Dear ________________:

I'd like to begin by thanking you for the role you've played in helping ____________ (name of child) to succeed at school each day. In recent months however, I have become increasingly concerned about ______________'s (name of child) difficulty with ____________________________________ (list areas of concern here).   Despite all of ___________'s (name of child) hard work in school and at home, ____________(his/her) grades are steadily declining.

I understand that I have the right to request that the school take steps to formally evaluate my child's abilities and present level of performance. Please contact me as soon as possible to advise me on the next step in this evaluation process. Thank you.

Sincerely,

(Your signature)

PRESENT LEVEL OF PERFORMANCE
SAMPLE LETTER

Date:

Re: (name of child)

Purpose of letter (present level of performance)

Dear ________________:

A few months have passed since our last meeting. I wanted to take this opportunity to share some of ______________'s (name of child) current strengths, areas of weakness and areas that he/she is making progress in. We have obtained an independent educational evaluation of __________'s (name of child) present level of functioning, which I will share with everyone when the team reconvenes on ___________ (date of next IEP or Child Study team Meeting). In the home environment, ____________(name of child) is doing a great job with the responsibility of caring for ___________(his/her) new pet. We are so proud of ___________(him/her)! _______________(name of child) continues to have sleeping difficulty, but we have noticed a slight improvement in the past few days with the implementation of an evening schedule and a firm bed time.

I'm looking forward to our meeting. Thank you so much for your commitment to ______________(name of child) and for helping her to do her best each day at school!

Sincerely,

(Your signature)

REQUEST FOR MEDICAL RECORDS - SAMPLE LETTER

Date:

To: (name of medical provider)

    (name of treatment facility and address)

Re: (name of child)

Date(s) of visit(s):

Purpose of letter: (request for medical record)

To Those Concerned:

My name is ______________________. My child,
_______________ (name of child) was treated in your office on the date(s) referenced above.

Please send me a copy of any progress or office notes and testing results that are in my child's medical chart for the dates referenced above. If there is a fee associated with the copying of records, please let me know as soon as possible. My contact information is below.

Thanks so much for your help!

Your name:

Home phone number:

Cell phone number:

Email address:

Best time to contact:

Sincerely,

(Your signature)

Appendix B: Whispers of Hope

Old Testament Scriptures (KJV)

Thou preparest a table before me in the presence of mine enemies: thou anointest my head with oil; my cup runneth over. Surely goodness and mercy shall follow me all the days of my life and I shall dwell in the house of the Lord for ever - Psalm 23:5-6

~~~~~~

He that dwelleth in the secret place of the most High shall abide under the shadow of the Almighty. I will say of the Lord, He is my refuge and my fortress: my God; in him will I trust - Psalm 91:1-2

~~~~~~

Trust in the Lord with all thine heart; and lean not unto thine own understanding. In all thy ways acknowledge him, and he shall direct thy paths. - Proverbs 3:5-6

~~~~~~

To everything there is a season, and a time to every purpose under the heaven... - Ecclesiastes 3:1

~~~~~~

He hath made everything beautiful in his time... - Ecclesiastes 3:11

~~~~~~

Surely he has borne our griefs, and carried our sorrows: yet we did esteem him stricken, smitten of God, and afflicted. But he was wounded for our transgressions; he was bruised for our iniquities: the chastisement of our peace was upon him; and with his stripes we are healed. - Isaiah 53:4-5
~~~~~~

For my thoughts are not your thoughts, neither are your ways my ways, saith the Lord. For as the heavens are higher than the earth, so are my ways higher than your ways, and my thoughts, than your thoughts. Isaiah 55:8

~ ~

Then said the Lord unto me, Thou hast well seen: for I will hasten my word to perform it. Jeremiah 1:12

~ ~

Before I formed thee in the belly, I knew thee; and before thou camest forth out of the womb I sanctified thee... Jeremiah 1:5

~ ~

Blessed is the man that trusteth in the Lord, and whose hope the Lord is. For he shall be as a tree planted by the waters, and that spreadeth out her roots by the river, and shall not see when heat cometh, but her leaf shall be green; and shall not be careful in the year of drought, neither shall cease from yielding fruit. - Jeremiah 17: 7-8

~ ~

For I know the thoughts that I think toward you, saith the Lord, thoughts of peace, and not of evil, to give you and expected end. - Jeremiah 29:11

~ ~

And I will restore to you the years that the locust hath eaten, the cankerworm, and the caterpillar, and the palmerworm, my great army which I sent among you. And ye shall eat in plenty, and be satisfied, and praise the name of the Lord your God, that hath dealt wondrously with you: and my people shall never be ashamed. Joel: 2:25-26

New Testament Scriptures (KJV)

But he answered and said, It is written, Man shall not live by bread alone, but by every word that proceedeth out of the mouth of God. Matthew 4:4

~ ~

But seek ye first the kingdom of God, and his righteousness... Take therefore no thought for the morrow: for the morrow shall take thought for the things of itself... Matthew 6:33(a) - 34(a)

~ ~

Come unto me, all ye that labour and are heavy laden, and I will give you rest. Take my yoke upon you, and learn of me; for I am meek and lowly in heart: and ye shall find rest for your souls. For my yoke is easy and my burden is light. Matthew 11:28-30

~ ~

And I will give unto thee the keys of the kingdom of heaven: and whatsoever thou shalt bind on earth shall be bound in heaven: and whatsoever thou shalt loose on earth shall be loosed in heaven. Matthew 16:19

~ ~

For where two or three are gathered in my name, there am I in the midst of them. Matthew 18:20

~ ~

Jesus said unto him, If thou canst believe, all things are possible to him that believeth. Mark 9:23

~ ~

Therefore I say unto you, What things soever ye desire, when ye pray, believe that ye receive them, and ye shall have them. Mark 11:24

For every one that asketh receiveth; and he that seeketh findeth; and to him that knocketh it shall be opened. Luke 11:10

~ ~

If ye abide in me and my words abide in you, ye shall ask what ye will, and it shall be done unto you. John 15:7

~ ~

These things I have spoken unto you, that in me ye might have peace. In the world, ye shall have tribulation: but be of good cheer; I have overcome the world. John 16:33

~ ~

He (Abraham) staggered not at the promise of God through unbelief; but was strong in faith, giving glory to God. And being fully persuaded that, what he had promised, he was able also to perform. Romans 4:20-21

~ ~

And we know that all things work together for good to them that love God, to them who are the called according to his purpose. Romans 8:28

~ ~

So then faith cometh by hearing, and hearing by the Word of God. Romans 10:7

~ ~

But as it is written, Eye hath not seen, nor ear heard, neither have entered into the heart of man, the things which God hath prepared for them that love him. I Corinthians2:9

~ ~

Therefore, my beloved brethren, be ye steadfast, unmovable, always abounding in the work of the Lord... I Corinthians 15:8

~ ~

For all the promises of God in him are yea, and in him Amen, unto the glory of God by us. II Corinthians 1:20

We are troubled on every side, yet not distressed; we are perplexed, but not in despair; Persecuted but not forsaken; cast down but not destroyed;   II Corinthians 4:8-9

~ ~

Now unto him that is able to do exceeding abundantly above all that we ask or think, according to the power that worketh in us... Ephesians 3:20

~ ~

Being confident of this very thing, that he which hath begun a good work in you will perform it until the day of Jesus Christ... Philippians 1:6

~ ~

Be careful (anxious) for nothing; but in every thing by prayer and supplication with thanksgiving let your requests be made known unto God. And the peace of God, which passeth all understanding, shall keep your hearts and minds through Christ Jesus. Philippians 4:6-7

~ ~

But my God shall supply all your need according to his riches in glory by Christ Jesus. Philippians 4:19

~ ~

Every good gift and every perfect gift is from above, and cometh down from the Father of lights, with whom is no variableness, neither shadow of turning. James 1: 17

~ ~

Appendix C:
Order Form

Order additional copies of

Helps, Hints and Hope

ORDER FORM

NAME: ____

ADDRESS: _____________________________________

CITY: ________________STATE: ___ZIP CODE: _____

PHONE: (H) ______________(W) ___________________

E-MAIL ADDRESS: _______________________________

	(Please allow 2 - 3 weeks for delivery.)		
Quantity	**Product Description**	**Price each**	**Total**
	Title: Helps, Hints and Hope	$12.95	

Total Order	$	
Shipping & Handling	$ 4.50	
Virginia Sales Tax: 5.0%	$	
Grand Total	$	

METHOD OF PAYMENT: ☐ *CASH* ☐*CHECK* ☐ *MONEYORDER*

MAKE CHECK PAYABLE TO: Rhema Designs, LLC

Mail Payment to: Rhema Designs, LLC

P.O. Box 85 Mechanicsville, VA. 23111

Credit Card: ☐VISA   ☐MasterCard

Number: ______________________________ Exp.___________

Signature___________________________________ CVC: _________

CONTACT US: Email: rhemadesignsllc@yahoo.com

On the web: www.rhemadesigns.org

Blog: www.faithoverdisability.blogspot.com